We Can Fi

by Beth Singer

A street has a big pit.

Can you fix it?

We can fix it!

We can dig and dig.

We can get six bags.

We can mix and mix.

We can fill the pit. Kids can play!

A street has a little hole.

Can you fix it?

We can dig and dig.

We can mix and mix.

We can fix it! Cars can go.